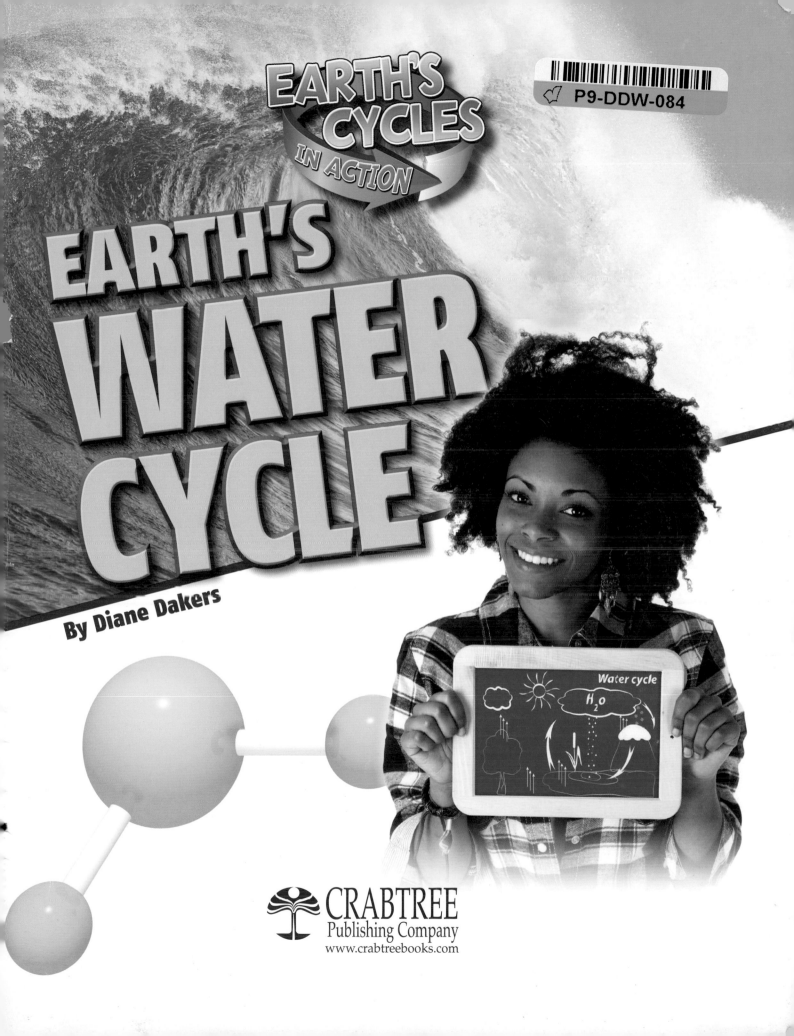

EARTH'S CYCLES IN ACTION

# EARTH'S WATER CYCLE

By Diane Dakers

Water cycle
H₂O

CRABTREE
Publishing Company
www.crabtreebooks.com

![Crabtree Publishing Company logo]

# Crabtree Publishing Company
### www.crabtreebooks.com

**Author:** Diane Dakers
**Publishing plan research and development:**
    Reagan Miller
**Project coordinator:** Mark Sachner,
    Water Buffalo Books
**Editors:** Mark Sachner, Shirley Duke
**Proofreader:** Shannon Welbourn
**Editorial director:** Kathy Middleton
**Photo researcher:** Ruth Owen
**Designer:** Westgraphix/Tammy West
**Contributing writer and indexer:** Suzy Gazlay
**Production coordinator and prepress technician:**
    Margaret Amy Salter
**Print coordinator:** Katherine Berti
**Science, reading, and curriculum consultant:**
    Suzy Gazlay, M.A.; Recipient, Presidential Award
    for Excellence in Science Teaching

Written, developed, and produced by
Water Buffalo Books

**Photographs and reproductions:**
**Front Cover: Shutterstock:** Max Topchii

**Interior: Alamy:** pp. 37, 40. **Corbis:** pp. 25, 27
(bottom), 30, 31, 34 (top left), 35, 36, 38.
**FLPA:** p. 23. **FogQuest/Pablo Osses:** p. 41.
**Suzy Gazlay:** pp. 42 (lower left and right),
43 (upper left and right, center left and right).
**NASA:** pp. 4, 5 (bottom).
**Public Domain:** p. 27 (top).
**Science Photo Library:** pp. 10 (bottom), 16 (left).
**Shutterstock:** pp. 1, 3, 5 (top), 6, 7, 8, 9, 10 (top), 11, 12,
13, 14, 15, 16 (right), 17, 18, 19, 20,
21, 22, 26, 28, 29, 32, 33, 34 (top right), 34 (bottom), 39,
42 (background, upper right),
43 (background, lower right), 44–45, 46.
**Shutterstock:** Chris Dorney: p. 13 (top left).

**Library and Archives Canada Cataloguing in Publication**

Dakers, Diane, author
    Earth's water cycle / Diane Dakers.

(Earth's cycles in action)
Includes index.
Issued in print and electronic formats.
ISBN 978-0-7787-0617-5 (bound).--ISBN 978-0-7787-0625-0 (pbk.).--
ISBN 978-1-4271-7627-1 (pdf).--ISBN 978-1-4271-7623-3 (html)

    1. Hydrologic cycle--Juvenile literature. I. Title.

GB848.D35 2014          j551.48          C2014-903936-0
                                         C2014-903937-9

**Library of Congress Cataloging-in-Publication Data**

Dakers, Diane.
  Earth's water cycle / Diane Dakers.
      pages cm -- (Earth's cycles in action)
  Includes index.
  ISBN 978-0-7787-0617-5 (reinforced library binding) --
ISBN 978-0-7787-0625-0 (pbk.) --
ISBN 978-1-4271-7627-1 (electronic pdf) --
ISBN 978-1-4271-7623-3 (electronic html)
  1. Hydrologic cycle--Juvenile literature. I. Title.

GB848.D35 2015
551.48--dc23

                              2014032600

# Crabtree Publishing Company
www.crabtreebooks.com          1-800-387-7650

Printed in Canada / 102014 / EF20140925

**Published
in Canada
Crabtree Publishing**
616 Welland Ave.
St. Catharines, Ontario
L2M 5V6

**Published in
the United States
Crabtree Publishing**
PMB 59051
350 Fifth Ave., 59th Floor
New York, NY 10118

**Published in the
United Kingdom
Crabtree Publishing**
Maritime House
Basin Road North, Hove
BN41 1WR

**Published
in Australia
Crabtree Publishing**
3 Charles Street
Coburg North
VIC, 3058

# Contents

Solid   Liquid   Gas

Water molecule

Oxygen   H₂O   Hydrogen

# CHAPTER 1

# Water, Water Everywhere

Water is all around us. About 70 percent of Earth is covered with water. Look at a photo of the planet from space. All the blue parts are water. That's why Earth is sometimes called the "blue planet." Water is the most **abundant**, or plentiful, substance on Earth, and one of the most important.

## Water World

About 97 percent of all the water on Earth is contained in five oceans— the Atlantic, Pacific, Indian, Arctic, and Antarctic. Ocean water is salt water. Only about 3 percent of the planet's water is **fresh water**. That's the kind of water that people and animals drink.

About two-thirds of Earth's fresh water is not available to drink because it is frozen as ice in the Arctic and in Antarctica. Just one-third of all fresh water is found in rivers and lakes and underground. This adds up to only about one percent of all the world's water being available as drinking water.

This photo from space shows Earth's western hemisphere. It also dramatically illustrates why we call our world, which is 70 percent covered with water, the "blue planet." The clouds that swirl around the planet are also filled with water. They play a major role in Earth's weather patterns and in the water cycle.

Water is the only substance on Earth that naturally exists in three states—solid, liquid, and gas.

*Solid* water takes the form of ice or snow. In addition to the ice and snow around Earth's North and South Poles, glaciers and icebergs are made of solid water.

*Liquid* water is what fills our oceans, lakes, rivers, and streams. Water also soaks into the ground, where gravity pulls it deeper and deeper.

This underground water is called **groundwater**.

Water exists as a *gas* in our air. In this form, it is called **water vapor**. Up to four percent of our air is made of **gaseous** water, or water vapor. This amount varies from day to day, and place to place.

Sea ice

Arctic Ocean

Above: This photo of an iceberg in Antarctica shows water in all three of its states: liquid (blue sea), solid (the iceberg), and gas (invisible water vapor in the air). Inset: Earth's North Pole is covered with floating sea ice over the Arctic Ocean.

You can't see water vapor, or smell it, or taste it, but sometimes you can feel it. On a hot, muggy day, it is the water vapor that makes the air feel humid, clammy, or "damp." Another way you can tell that liquid water has turned into water vapor is to hang wet laundry on the clothesline. Eventually, the laundry is no longer wet. That's because the liquid water has turned into vapor and escaped into the air.

The only time you can "see" water vapor is when a lot of it collects in one place and starts to cool. At that point, water vapor turns into steam. For example, when a tea kettle boils, a tiny cloud of steam comes out of the spout. That's because the hot water in the kettle quickly turns to vapor, collects in a small area, and immediately begins to cool. The steam is actually a collection of tiny water droplets floating in the air.

When wet laundry hanging on a clothesline dries, water has gone from a liquid to a gas in the form of water vapor.

The steam coming out of this tea kettle is actually a tiny cloud of water droplets. It forms when water vapor from within the kettle comes into contact with cooler air outside of the kettle.

## States of Water

Everything in the world is made up of **atoms** and **molecules**. Atoms are individual building blocks of matter, and molecules are combinations of those building blocks. The **Periodic Table of Elements** lists 118 known types of atoms. For example, one of those is hydrogen, represented on the periodic table as H. Another is oxygen, represented by the letter O. Water might look like a pretty simple substance, but it is actually made up of hydrogen and oxygen. When two hydrogen atoms combine with one oxygen atom, they form a molecule called $H_2O$. That is water.

Whether it is a solid, liquid, or gas, this structure basically never changes. Water is solid as ice when the temperature is below 32 degrees Fahrenheit (0 degrees Celsius). When it's warmer than that, ice melts and becomes liquid water.

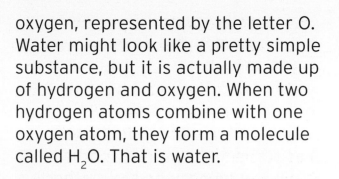

2 hydrogen atoms +
1 oxygen atom =
1 water molecule
($H_2O$)

The Periodic Table of Elements shows all the chemical **elements** known to exist. Some elements occur naturally, and others are developed in laboratories and are therefore artificial, or human-made. The periodic table lists them in order of increasing atomic number, or the number of **protons** in the atom's nucleus. Hydrogen is number 1 in the table. Oxygen is number 8.

## Periodic Table of Elements

| 1 IA / 1 A | | | | | | | | | | | | | | | | | 18 VIIIA / 8A |
|---|---|---|---|---|---|---|---|---|---|---|---|---|---|---|---|---|---|
| 1 1.00794 H Hidrogen | 2 IIA / 2A | | | | | | | | | | | 13 IIIA / 3A | 14 IVA / 4A | 15 VA / 5A | 16 VIA / 6A | 17 VIIA / 7A | 2 4.002602 He Helium |
| 3 6.941 Li Lithium | 4 9.012182 Be Beryllium | | | | | | | | | | | 5 10.811 B Boron | 6 12.0107 C Carbon | 7 14.0067 N Nitrogen | 8 15.9994 O Oxygen | 9 18.998403 F Fluorine | 10 20.1797 Ne Neon |
| 11 22.98977 Na Sodium | 12 24.3050 Mg Magnesium | 3 IIIB / 3B | 4 IVB / 4B | 5 VB / 5B | 6 VIB / 6B | 7 VIIB / 7B | 8 —VIII— 8 | 9 | 10 | 11 IB / 1B | 12 IIB / 2B | 13 26.98155 Al Aluminum | 14 28.0855 Si Silicon | 15 30.97696 P Phosphorus | 16 32.065 S Sulfur | 17 35.453 Cl Chlorine | 18 39.948 Ar Argon |
| 19 39.0983 K Potassium | 20 40.078 Ca Calcium | 21 44.95591 Sc Scandium | 22 47.867 Ti Titanium | 23 50.9415 V Vanadium | 24 51.9962 Cr Chromium | 25 54.93804 Mn Manganese | 26 55.845 Fe Iron | 27 58.93319 Co Cobalt | 28 58.6934 Ni Nickel | 29 63.546 Cu Copper | 30 65.38 Zn Zinc | 31 69.723 Ga Gallium | 32 72.64 Ge Germanium | 33 74.92160 As Arsenic | 34 78.96 Se Selenium | 35 79.904 Br Bromine | 36 83.798 Kr Kryptone |
| 37 85.4678 Rb Rubidium | 38 87.62 Sr Strontium | 39 88.90585 Y Yttrium | 40 91.224 Zr Zirconium | 41 92.90638 Nb Niobium | 42 95.96 Mo Molybdenum | 43 (98) Tc Technetium | 44 101.07 Ru Ruthenium | 45 102.9055 Rh Rhodium | 46 106.42 Pd Palladium | 47 107.8682 Ag Silver | 48 112.441 Cd Cadmium | 49 114.818 In Indium | 50 118.710 Sn Tin | 51 121.760 Sb Antimony | 52 127.60 Te Tellurium | 53 126.9044 I Iodine | 54 131.293 Xe Xenon |
| 55 132.9054 Cs Cesium | 56 137.327 Ba Barium | 57-71 | 72 178.49 Hf Hafnium | 73 180.9478 Ta Tantalum | 74 183.84 W Tungsten | 75 186.207 Re Rhenium | 76 190.23 Os Osmium | 77 192.217 Ir Iridium | 78 195.084 Pt Platinum | 79 196.9665 Au Gold | 80 200.59 Hg Mercury | 81 204.3833 Tl Thallium | 82 207.2 Pb Lead | 83 208.9804 Bi Bismuth | 84 (210) Po Polonium | 85 (210) At Astatine | 86 (220) Rn Radon |
| 87 (223) Fr Francium | 88 226.025 Ra Radium | 89-103 | 104 (261) Rf Rutherfordium | 105 (262) Db Dubnium | 106 (266) Sg Seaborgium | 107 (264) Bh Bohrium | 108 (277) Hs Hassium | 109 (268) Mt Meitnerium | 110 (271) Ds Darmstadtium | 111 (272) Rg Roentgenium | 112 (285) Cn Copernicum | 113 (284) Uut Ununtrium | 114 (289) Uuq Ununquadium | 115 (288) Uup Ununpentium | 116 (292) Uuh Ununhexium | 117 (294) Uus Ununseptium | 118 (294) Uuo Ununoctium |

Liquid water may become vapor in more than one way. In one process, liquid water heated to its boiling point of 212°F (100°C) will become vapor. When you watch a pot of boiling water, you see bubbles forming in the water. Those bubbles are water vapor surrounded by liquid water. The bubbles rise to the surface of the boiling liquid and escape into the air.

Another way liquid water becomes water vapor is through a process called **evaporation**. In every substance, molecules are in constant motion. In liquid water, $H_2O$ molecules zip around and sometimes crash into each other. When that happens at the water's surface, some molecules are knocked right out of the liquid and into the air!

Evaporation happens at the surface of every body of water, be it a glass of water, a puddle, or an ocean. It can happen at any temperature, as long as the water is in liquid form.

The crystal-clear waters of a babbling river, the salty ocean, and a stagnant mud puddle. All three bodies of water contain some form of salt, although only the ocean has enough for us to call it a "saltwater" body.

## Salty Water Everywhere

There are many kinds of salt on our planet, and all water contains some form of dissolved salt. When we drink a glass of water from the tap, though, it doesn't taste salty to us. One reason we can't taste salt is that it may not be the kind of salt most of us are used to putting on our food. Also, the amount of salt in fresh water is small compared to the amount of salt in seawater. In fact, ocean water is about 220 times as salty as lake or river water. That's a big reason it tastes so, well, salty!

Imagine all the rivers that drain into an ocean. Each of those rivers contains substances that include salt. When hundreds of rivers drain into an ocean, all those substances go into the ocean, too.

When water evaporates from the surface of an ocean, it is mostly the water itself that evaporates. Most of the salt, especially the salt that isn't dissolved into the water, stays behind.

Millions of years ago, seawater wasn't as salty as it is today. Over time, the salt **concentration**, meaning the amount of salt in the water, has built up to today's levels.

The warmer the water, the faster the molecules move, and the more quickly the water evaporates. As water freezes into solid ice, the molecules slow down.

## Our Body of Water

Water is all around us, but it's also inside us. Every human being is mostly made of water. Our water content ranges from about 60 to 75 percent, depending on a person's age, gender, and activity level, among other things.

Like other living things, however, we all need water to survive.

In animals, water keeps organs and body systems working properly. It distributes **nutrients** throughout a body and helps with the digestion of food. It also helps regulate, or control, body temperature, to make sure the animal doesn't get too hot or too cold. Bodily fluids, such as blood, are mostly water.

Most plants are 90 to 95 percent water. Plant cells are full of water.

In humans, blood is made up of red blood cells, which carry oxygen through the body; white blood cells, which help fight infections and disease; platelets, which help blood clot; and plasma, a liquid that carries nutrients and other essential substances in your blood, and in which the blood's cells and platelets are suspended. More than half our blood is made of plasma, which is mostly water. This means that our blood is about half water. So drink plenty of water—it's good for your blood!

Plasma

Red blood cells

White blood cells

Platelets

Their cell walls give the plant structure. Imagine a balloon filled with water. When it is full, it keeps its round shape. When the water starts to leak out, the balloon shrivels and collapses. That is similar to what happens if plant cells don't have enough water. The cells shrink, the cell walls are unable to push outward, and the plant wilts. That's why it's important to water your plants!

Like animals, plants need water to transport important minerals to all their cells. Plants also need water for a process called **photosynthesis**.

To get the water they need for all these functions, plants use their roots to draw water from the soil. But how does water get into the soil in the first place? And how does water get into lakes and streams so animals can drink it? That's where the water cycle comes in.

Leaf cells photographed by a microscope

Cell walls

Cell

Chloroplasts that produce the chemical chlorophyll, which is needed for photosynthesis to take place

## Green Power: Photosynthesis and Plants

Photosynthesis is a process that green plants use to make their food. For photosynthesis to happen, a plant needs three ingredients. One is water ($H_2O$). A plant's roots absorb water from the soil. The water travels up the stem and to the leaves. As the leaves are drawing water from within the plant, they are also collecting another key ingredient, carbon dioxide ($CO_2$) gas, from the air around the plant. Meanwhile, a chemical in the leaves called chlorophyll absorbs sunlight. With sunlight, the list of ingredients required for photosynthesis is complete.

Through chemical reactions in the plant's leaves, photosynthesis breaks down carbon dioxide and water and releases two new **compounds**. One is glucose ($C_6H_{12}O_6$), a type of sugar, which feeds the plant. The other is oxygen (O), which is released into the air. That oxygen keeps humans and other animals alive!

# Only a Few Drops to Drink

Most of the Earth is covered with water, but there are a few places that are actually quite dry. Most deserts, for example, are areas that don't get much rainfall. It's not that deserts have *no* water. They just have very little compared to other places on the planet.

In some deserts, water flows in underground springs. In others, water is frozen into ice and snow. Some deserts only get water when it rains once or twice a year. Some deserts have the occasional pocket of water called an **oasis**.

Plants and animals that live in a desert have adapted, or changed over periods of time to fit in with their environment. These organisms can live with less water. Some kinds of cactus—for example, barrel cactus (seen here)—can store enough water to live for two or more years! Other plants have extra-long roots that reach deep underground springs. Some animals that live in deserts get water by eating these plants. Some might fill up at an oasis, where they may also live off of plants that grow near the water.

In the United States, the population of some desert states, such as Arizona, New Mexico, and Nevada, is 10 times what it was 60 years ago. People have moved there because of the warm, sunny climate. All these new residents use water for drinking, laundry, bathing, watering the lawn, and maintaining golf courses. That drains the limited water sources and may threaten the delicate balance of a desert's natural ecosystem.

# CHAPTER 2

# Cycles Make the World Go 'Round

In the opening scenes of the movie *The Lion King*, Mustafa presents his new baby lion cub, Simba, to all the animals in the kingdom. Before long, King Mustafa dies, and young Simba runs away. Eventually, Simba grows up, becomes an adult lion, and returns to the land of his birth. There, Simba becomes king. The movie closes with King Simba presenting his newly born lion cub to the animals of the kingdom. The song "The Circle of Life" plays in the background.

*The Lion King* shows us a perfect example of a cycle. In this case, it's a life cycle. An animal is born, it grows up, has a baby, and eventually dies. The new baby grows up, has babies of its own ... and so on.

A cycle is a pattern of related processes or events that happens over and over again. Like a circle, a cycle has no beginning and ending. It just keeps going and going and going....

In just five years, this little cub will be the size of his father and will be ready to breed and produce cubs of his own.

Spring

Summer

Winter

Fall

## Cycles of Life

Every day, our planet performs many cycles. In fact, every day is a cycle, and so is every year. One very obvious cycle is the changing of the seasons. This cycle occurs as Earth orbits, or travels around, the Sun. Spring, summer, fall, winter. That's a cycle that happens over and over again, year after year.

The raindrops falling in this pond may have been part of an ocean wave just a few weeks ago.

## The Water Cycle

Some of Earth's cycles are quite complicated. The water cycle, for example, has many steps. Powered by energy from the Sun and by gravity, water is in constant motion. As a natural substance that cannot be created or destroyed, all the water that exists on the planet moves through its three states, cycling from Earth to the sky and back to Earth—again and again in a never-ending cycle.

# CHAPTER 3

# The Never–Ending Cycle

After a rainfall, water sits in a puddle. The puddle water eventually evaporates into the air, where water vapor cools, condenses, and collects into droplets and forms clouds, until it rains again. That's a super-simple version of the water cycle. The path of that puddle water is part of a never-ending cycle that is constantly moving all the water on our planet, from the sky to the Earth, and back to the sky. The cycle includes not only bodies of water, the land, and the sky, but also all of Earth's plants and animals. Let's look at the water cycle one step at a time, beginning with the biggest water source on the planet—the oceans.

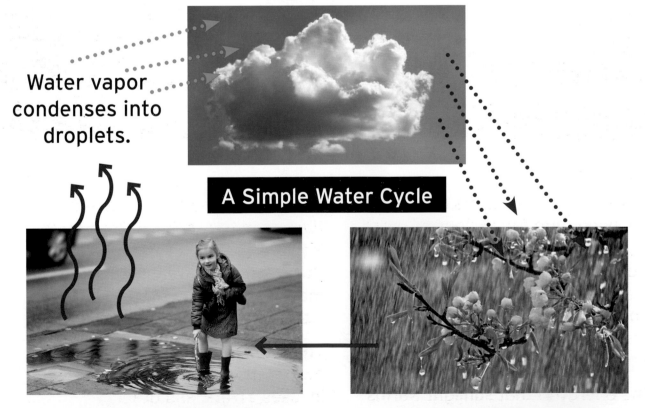

Water droplets form clouds.

Water vapor condenses into droplets.

A Simple Water Cycle

Water evaporates.

Droplets fall as rain.

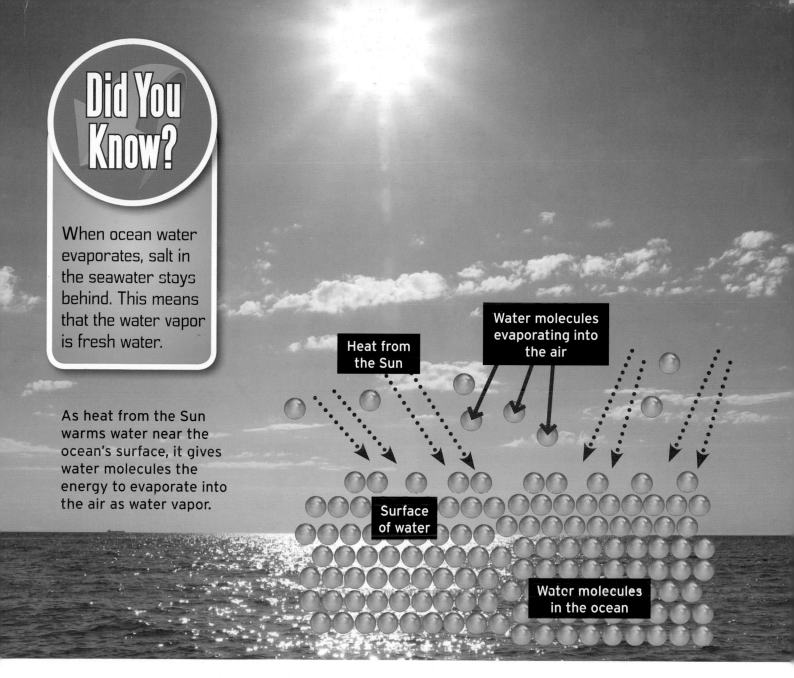

As heat from the Sun warms water near the ocean's surface, it gives water molecules the energy to evaporate into the air as water vapor.

Heat from the Sun

Water molecules evaporating into the air

Surface of water

Water molecules in the ocean

## Into the Air

All the water that exists on Earth has been here for millions of years. Even though water changes states, most of it is, and has always been, contained in liquid form in the world's oceans. The surface area of Earth's oceans is vast, so it absorbs a huge amount of sunlight every day.

The energy in that sunlight warms the seawater near the surface, giving water molecules the energy they need to escape, or evaporate, into the air. The warmer the air, the warmer the water, and the more liquid converts to gas, or water vapor.

This step in the water cycle is evaporation, and it also happens in lakes, rivers, and other freshwater bodies.

This isn't the only way that liquid water becomes water vapor, though. Remember that plants contain a lot of water, too! A plant takes in water from the soil through its roots. The water then travels up the stem and to all parts of the plant, eventually reaching the leaves. From there, some of the water evaporates through small holes, or pores, on the underside of the leaves, moving into the air. This process, by which water travels from the roots throughout the plant and then evaporates through the leaves, is called **transpiration**.

**Dandelion plant**

**Stomata**

**Roots**

The small pores on the underside of a plant's leaves are called stomata. Each leaf has thousands of stomata. Water vapor is released through these holes during transpiration.

## From Ice to Vapor

Water may also change into water vapor through a process called **sublimation**.

Even in ice, water molecules are in constant motion. They just move more slowly when water is in its solid state. Still, some of the molecules at the surface of ice will eventually escape. During sublimation, some of the molecules change from snow or ice directly to water vapor, without melting into water first. When it's windy, or when the Sun is shining, sublimation happens faster. This is why, on bitterly cold, bright sunny days, ice often disappears from sidewalks and highways.

During deposition, water vapor comes into contact with a cold window pane and changes to frost, creating these beautiful patterns.

Sublimation also happens in your freezer! Look at a tray of shrunken ice cubes that have been left in the freezer for a really long time. They have shrunk because of sublimation. There is no liquid water in the ice tray, but the ice cubes are smaller. That's because the water molecules in the ice have transformed directly into water vapor.

In the opposite process, water vapor changes directly into ice, such as snowflakes or frost, without first becoming a liquid. This process, called **deposition**, also occurs when temperatures are very cold.

## What Goes Up Must Come Down

Once water vapor is in the air, wind moves it around and lifts it high into the sky. Thanks to the wind, water vapor can travel a long way from where it started! As the vapor rises, it cools and forms tiny droplets of water. This transformation from water vapor to liquid water is called **condensation**.

High in the chilly sky, droplets bump into each other and join together to form bigger droplets. They also form around dust, pollen, and other particles that attract the water droplets. These particles help water vapor condense faster.

When billions of these droplets join together, they form clouds. Eventually, the water droplets become too heavy to stay in the air. Gravity pulls them toward Earth, and they fall as rain.

Water droplets

Tiny water droplets form bigger droplets, which eventually form clouds. These photos show clouds of various sizes, shapes, **altitude**, and moisture content.

# Dew Drops

Sometimes, when you get up in the morning, you see water droplets on the grass or on spider webs. Those drops are called **dew**. Dew is formed by the condensation of water vapor in the air. When the air cools down at night, some of that water vapor condenses and becomes liquid water. In the morning, the water has collected into the little droplets you see.

If the temperature in the cloud is below the freezing point of water, the vapor in the air forms ice crystals instead of water droplets. These tiny ice crystals bond together to form larger crystals. When these crystals become too heavy to stay in the cloud, they fall as snow. Under some weather conditions, rain and partially melted snow may become a slushy, wintery mix. In other conditions, water may freeze into ice pellets, sometimes called sleet. These pellets make tapping or "hissing" sounds as they hit objects on the ground.

Ice may also strike the ground in the form of hail. Hail usually occurs during warmer times of the year, when thunderstorms carry droplets high into the **atmosphere**. There, the temperatures are cold enough for droplets to join together as they freeze and form hailstones. The size depends on how much water freezes around it before it falls to the ground. We sometimes hear hail banging on cars and roofs during the summer!

The various forms of rain and ice crystals falling from the sky are all types of **precipitation**, the name of this part of the water cycle.

A photo of precipitation in the form of ice crystals bonded together in larger crystals out of supercooled water droplets—better known to most of us as snow!

## Underground Water

Once water has fallen back to Earth as precipitation, it has to go somewhere before it starts to evaporate and begin the cycle all over again. This step in the cycle is called **collection**.

Because 70 percent of our planet is covered with water, most of the precipitation ends up back in those bodies of water—oceans, lakes, rivers, and streams. Some, though, falls onto land.

In certain regions, the water trickles down hillsides, mountains, and slopes until it runs into a river or lake. This water is called **runoff**, and sooner or later it finds its way back to an ocean.

In cities, this runoff cannot soak into pavement, so it flows into storm drains, which carry it away through the sewer system. Or it settles in puddles, which evaporate after the rain stops.

About 20 percent of water that falls to Earth soaks into the ground. It seeps through the top layers of soil and is pulled deeper by the force of gravity.

## MAKING SENSE OF CYCLES

Clouds come in different sizes, shapes, and colors, and they can be found at many different altitudes, or heights. For example, fog is a cloud that is close to the ground. The size and shape of a cloud may depend on temperature and wind in the sky, as well as how high the cloud is. Based on facts and pictures in this book, think about why certain clouds might be different colors and shapes. What do you think makes some clouds thin and wispy, and others heavy looking, and some almost completely white and others very dark?

The water in this spectacular waterfall in Norway started out as precipitation falling to Earth and collecting into small mountain streams. As shown here, those streams flow into larger rivers, which eventually find their way to the sea.

# Watering the Animals

All animals, including humans, need water to survive. Many animals get it by drinking fresh water or by eating plants, which contain water. Water constantly circulates throughout an organism, bringing nutrition and energy to every organ and cell in every part of the body. It eventually leaves the organism and returns to the water cycle. Humans and other mammals sweat, which releases water into the air—and, therefore, into the water cycle. Mammals and other types of animals, even insects, also urinate, which releases liquid water into the water cycle. Fish take in and get rid of water through their gills. Other animals, such as frogs and lizards, absorb and release moisture through their skin. Every type of animal has to get rid of waste material somehow, and they all do it in different ways!

## The Water Cycle

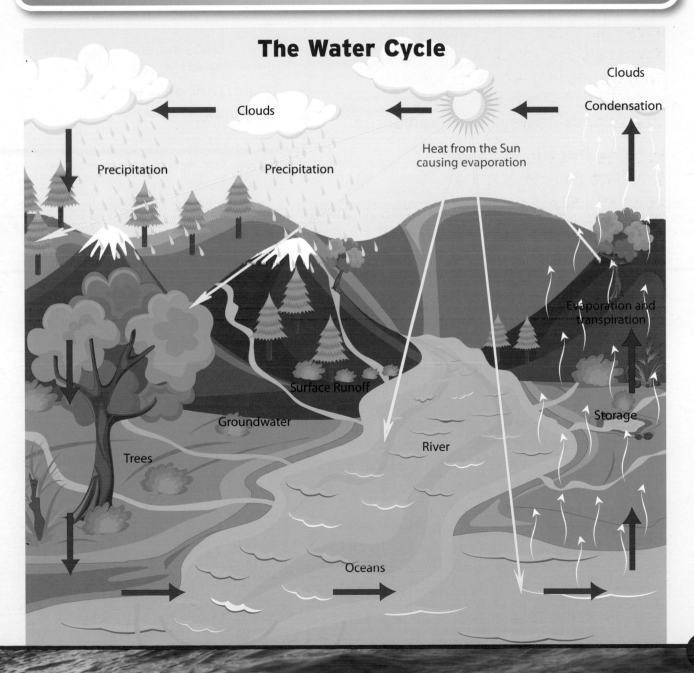

Eventually, the water reaches a level called the **water table**. The depth of the water table varies from location to location. Above the water table, the underground water trickles around rocks, stones, and sand, flowing downward.

Below the water table, every crack, pore, and air pocket in the ground is completely filled with water. This area is called the **saturated** zone, because it is saturated with, or full of, groundwater.

This is a source of drinking water for many people around the world. They dig wells, searching for an **aquifer** in the saturated zone. An aquifer is an underground area that contains a great deal of groundwater—enough to serve the people of a community, or to irrigate farmland.

What happens, though, if there is no groundwater? Or if the groundwater runs out, and there are no rivers and lakes? What do people do for clean drinking water, and to help them grow food? This is a problem that millions of people around the globe face every day.

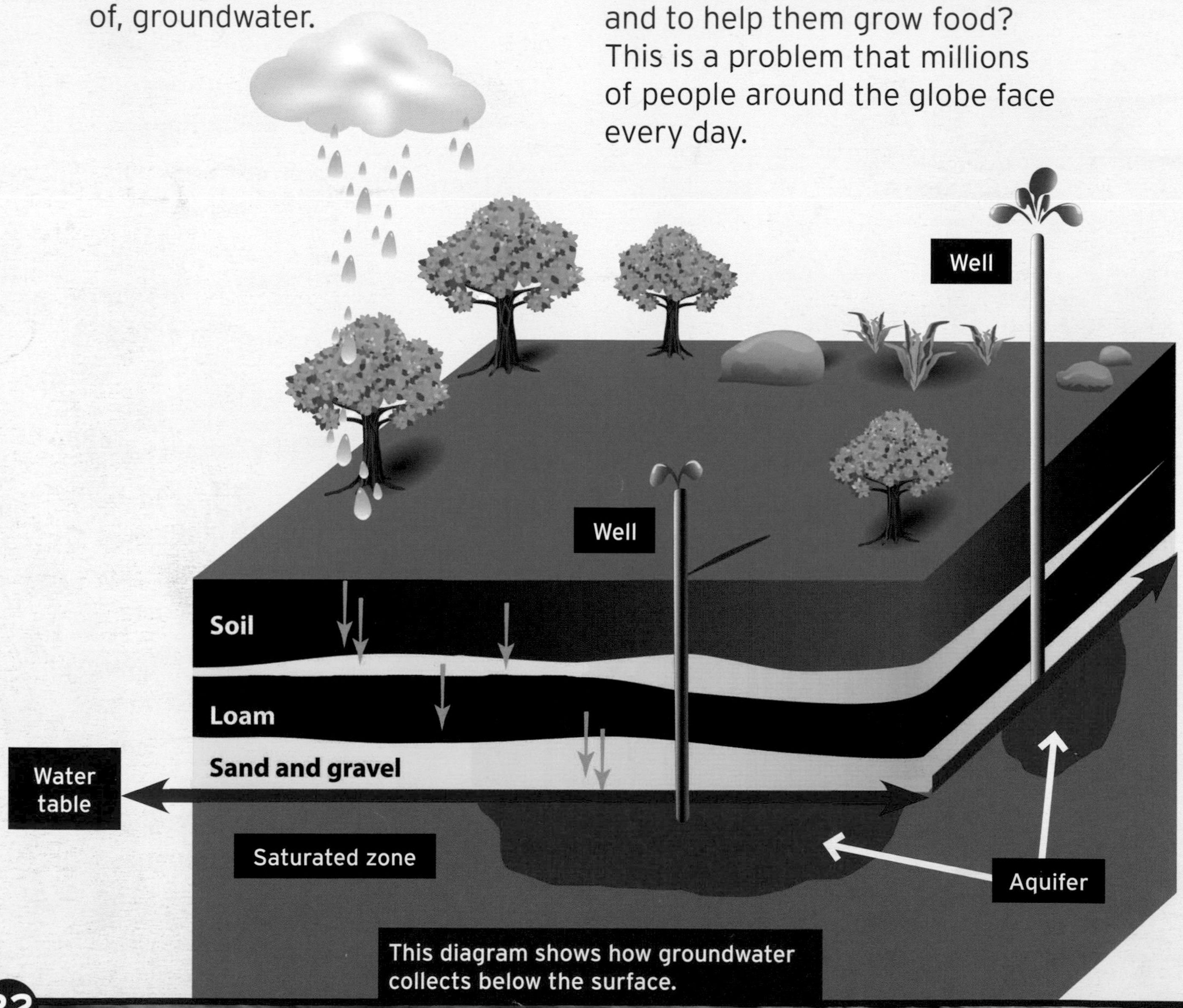

Well

Well

Soil

Loam

Sand and gravel

Water table

Saturated zone

Aquifer

This diagram shows how groundwater collects below the surface.

# In Hot Water

The deeper underground that groundwater goes, the hotter it gets. Sometimes groundwater is pulled so deep into Earth's crust that its temperature can reach the boiling point. In some places, this water then returns to the surface in pools called hot springs.

Sometimes, a cold spring feeds into the same pool. This cools down the water, so people can enjoy soaking in the hot spring. Sometimes, people add cooler water to control the heat. In other cases, as the hot water circulates back to the surface, it naturally cools down again, making the hot spring a suitable temperature for human relaxation.

It's not only people who enjoy soaking in hot springs. In Japan, macaque monkeys warm up in hot springs during the cold, snowy winter.

# CHAPTER 4

# Water Woes

In some parts of the world, we take water for granted. We turn on the kitchen tap, and clean water comes out. We have plenty of water for drinking, cooking, growing food, washing, watering the lawn, and bathing the dog. About one-third of the world's population isn't so lucky. Some people have no fresh water near their homes. Other people have access to water, but it is not clean enough to drink or wash in.

## Lack of Water Times Two

There are two main reasons that people don't have enough fresh water. One is called physical **scarcity**. That means there is simply not enough water in a particular place. This can happen when lack of rainfall leads to **drought**. The overuse of water supplies due to population increases also contributes to physical scarcity. The other reason people lack water is economic scarcity. That means the water is there, but the people or government can't afford to build a well or pump to reach it. Or they can't afford a system to clean it or pipes to transport it to the people who need it.

In some places, people have to walk miles every day to reach a river or a well to get fresh water. Then they carry home full jugs or cans that can weigh as much as 40 pounds (18 kilograms). That's about how much two average car tires weigh. Imagine walking for miles in the heat carrying two tires!

## Running Dry

In some parts of the world, rivers, lakes, and underground water sources are running dry. That's because water is being used faster than the water cycle can replace it in those areas. Very hot and dry parts of the world are in particular danger of running out of water. Areas in the Middle East, Asia, and Africa face the greatest risk right now.

## Lack of Water Facts

- About 800,000 people around the world live in areas without enough water.
- Earth's population is three times greater today than it was 100 years ago; water use is six times greater.
- Twice as much of Earth's land faces drought today, compared to 30 years ago.
- Two-thirds of China's cities suffer from water shortages.
- About 40 percent of people in Africa live in areas where water is scarce.
- Water for agriculture and food production uses about 70 percent of the world's fresh water supplies.
- Americans use more water per household than people in any other country on Earth.
- Water is considered such a precious resource that in the past, countries have fought wars over who could use the water in certain rivers.

A group of women and girls carrying buckets of water in Tanzania, East Africa.

# Water Supply

Drinking-water supplies for cities and towns come from two sources—**surface water** and groundwater.

Surface water is, literally, water on Earth's surface. Lakes, streams, and rivers are examples of surface water sources. Surface water is often directed into a **reservoir**, or artificial lake. There, it is stored to make sure there will be a plentiful supply of fresh water for the town or city, even if it doesn't rain for a long time.

Groundwater, on the other hand, is water that has pooled deep underground. This water must be pumped to the surface before it can be used as a water supply. In rural areas, individual homes might have private wells for this purpose. A larger town might have a community well that serves the whole population. In this case, well water might be directed into a reservoir, or it might be stored in a water tank or water tower. Water tanks and towers are usually located high above the ground. From there, gravity helps pump the water into a system that brings it to homes, schools, hospitals, and other buildings.

## Problems Closer to Home

Lack of water isn't just a problem in faraway places. In California, for example, the water shortage has reached a crisis point. In January 2014, after years of record low rain and snowfall, the governor declared a drought state of emergency. By the summer of 2014, river and reservoir levels had reached all-time lows.

California has the highest population of any U.S. state. More than 38 million people live there, and all those people need water. This demand has stressed the natural water cycle. One response to this demand, and one of the main causes of the water crisis in rural parts of the state, has been the diverting, or rerouting, of water from its natural course.

The Hetch Hetchy Reservoir is an artificial lake in Yosemite National Park that provides water to the San Francisco Bay area. The water travels about 167 miles (270 km) through a gravity-fed pipe system.

Water tanks, like the one shown here, draw water from underground and use gravity to pump it to the surrounding community.

This sends water into areas where it doesn't naturally flow, such as the heavily populated areas around San Francisco Bay and in Southern California. It also takes water from areas where water once flowed abundantly.

To get water to cities, people sometimes build dams to change the natural flow of rivers.

The Colorado River, for example, supplies water for people in seven different states, including California. Not only is this water used for drinking and cooking, it is used to fill swimming pools, wash cars, and water lawns and golf courses. The Colorado River has been dammed and drained to the point that it has actually run dry in some places.

For six million years, the Colorado River naturally drained into the Gulf of California, which is in Mexico, not far from the U.S. border. It stopped doing that in 1998. The river now dries up before it gets to the sea!

It's not just lack of water that causes problems around the world, though. Some places have water—people just can't drink it because it is so dirty or polluted.

This map shows the path of the Colorado River from its headwaters in the Rocky Mountains to its mouth in the Gulf of California, in Mexico. As this photo dramatically illustrates, after supplying water to vast areas of the U.S. Southwest along its route, the river is dry or a trickle by the time it reaches the sea along the border of the Mexican states of Sonora and Baja California.

# CHAPTER 5

# Dirty Water

All the water that has ever existed still exists today. For millions of years, it has traveled through the various steps of the water cycle, over and over again. In addition to moving water around the planet and changing its state from solid to liquid to gas, the water cycle also cleans the water. Today, though, natural processes aren't enough. The water cycle can't keep up with all the damage that humans are doing to the world's water supply.

Melting glacial ice brings fresh, pure water to this mountain stream.

Chemical reactions with oxygen in the air help purify the water in this stream.

## Naturally Clean

The water cycle naturally purifies, or cleans, all the water on Earth. When ocean water evaporates, it leaves the salt and other **impurities** behind. This produces pure water vapor. The water in icebergs, glaciers, and Arctic ice fields has been frozen for millions of years. It is clean, pure water. When it melts, that clean water enters the water cycle.

When runoff trickles over rocks, chemicals in the water react with oxygen in the air and form new compounds. As these compounds are near the surface of the water, they are released into the atmosphere, leaving behind pure water.

## MAKING SENSE OF CYCLES

We know that water changes between solid, liquid, and vapor (or gaseous) states. When we think of the water cycle, we usually think of two paths, or steps. One takes water molecules from a liquid to a gaseous state, and the other takes them from a gas to a liquid. Besides these two paths, however, there are many other paths that water molecules might take through the water cycle.

Use information that you have taken from this book, as well as your own experiences, to describe at least seven paths that water molecules might take through a water cycle. We'll start you off with two of the most familiar paths: (1) from liquid in the ocean to vapor in the sky, and (2) from vapor to liquid in the form of water droplets in a cloud. What other paths can you add to these? (Remember, water may exist in three states!)

Many **aquatic** plants, such as these rushes, help purify water. They can even remove harmful bacteria and substances such as oil from water.

In soil, tiny organisms, called microbes or microorganisms, break down other impurities in water. These microorganisms, which can only be seen with a microscope, use the substances for food. As this process occurs, the water is purified. In slow-moving rivers and lakes, large particles settle to the bottom, clearing them out of the water. Sand is also a natural water filter. Plants, too, purify water that cycles through them.

## When Nature Can't Keep Up

As Earth's population increases, more and more people are using—and polluting—water. The water cycle cannot clean it fast enough. Most cities, towns, and rural communities have water purification systems to make sure their citizens have enough clean water.

A purification system first screens the water to remove large objects such as plants, garbage, and dirt.

With no access to modern waste disposal systems, these young boys must dispose of raw sewage in a stream running through their poverty-stricken neighborhood in Nairobi, the capital city of Kenya, Africa.

The water is then treated with a number of other processes that remove chemicals, harmful bacteria, germs, **parasites**, and other tiny impurities.

For millions of people around the world, though, water purification systems are not available or they cost too much. Without a clean water supply, these people are forced to drink water that is unsafe. They end up drinking and washing in water that is **contaminated**, or polluted, with human and animal waste, chemicals, harmful bacteria, insects, and worms.

People get sick and many die because they lack safe drinking water. Children are particularly at risk.

One of the greatest threats to the world's water supply is raw sewage, or human waste. When you flush a toilet, the dirty water might go into a sewer system. Sometimes, it is cleaned before it goes back into the water system. Sometimes, though, it is just dumped in a river or ocean.

Some homes are on septic systems. That means the sewage goes underground. There, it might go into a holding tank. Or it might just go into the soil and eventually end up in the groundwater.

## Dirty Details

- More people in the world have cell phones than access to toilets.
- More than one billion people in the world do not have sanitation systems that separate sewage from water.
- A child somewhere in the world dies from a water-related illness very 21 seconds.
- Worldwide, more than 800,000 children under age five die from diarrhea every year. Most of these deaths are related to unsafe drinking water.
- Half of the world's hospital beds are filled with people suffering from water-related illnesses.

In many of the world's poorest countries, raw sewage is not separated from drinking water. Just imagine what people living in these places must put into their bodies when they take a bath or drink water. Not only is the thought of drinking or preparing food in sewage disgusting, but the germs in waste matter can cause terrible diseases.

## Unnaturally Dirty

As the world's population rises, so do the threats to our water systems. All of these threats involve upsetting the balance of the water cycle. One problem is overuse of water. Another huge concern is water pollution. It can change the chemistry of water, threaten marine life, and make people sick.

River pollution from rows of shanty houses in Manila, Philippines.

Pollution comes from all kinds of sources. Sometimes, it is obvious. For example, when you see a plastic bag floating down a river, you know that bag doesn't belong there. Another time, you might see a shiny coating of oil or gasoline on the water's surface. Clearly, that is not a natural part of the body of water, either. As water flows from lakes to rivers to oceans, it carries **pollutants** like garbage, plastics, oil, and other toxic materials from one place to another. The pollutants can be spread over long distances.

Some types of water pollution aren't this obvious, though. Chemicals, for example, pose a great danger to waterways and people, but you usually can't see them by looking at the water.

In cities, rain can rinse chemicals off roads and parking lots and into storm drains. These storm drains lead to local waterways. Sometimes people pour things like paints, detergents, and cleaning products down a drain or into a roadside gutter. These, too, can end up in local waterways.

Many industries use chemicals that find their way into our water. Mining, manufacturing, food processing, mills that pulp, or grind, wood products, and many other industries produce wastewater. Often this water is contaminated with chemicals.

A river polluted by chemicals from a copper mining operation. Despite laws to limit dumping chemical wastewater, and even when mining has stopped, water can flood an abandoned mine, mix with chemicals, and cause toxic waste to flow into nearby water sources.

It's not just garbage and chemicals that threaten our water. Water that is warmer than it is supposed to be also harms marine life. This is called **thermal pollution**.

Some factories and power plants suck cold water out of streams and lakes. They use it to cool down machinery. It's a cheap way to keep equipment from overheating and breaking down.

Unfortunately, plants, fish, and other aquatic animals may be sucked up and killed during this process. In addition, when the water is returned to the waterway, it is warmer than when it was taken out. Certain species of plants and animals are not adapted to these warmer temperatures. Even a couple of degrees difference might mean some of these species can no longer live in a particular area.

Warmer water also contains less oxygen—and just about all animals need oxygen to survive. Less oxygen means some animal species will move away or die off. This changes the entire ecosystem in the water.

Many countries have laws preventing companies from dumping this wastewater. They are required to clean wastewater in a water treatment facility before releasing it into the environment.

Unfortunately, there are more countries in the world *without* such laws than countries that have them. In these places, factories and other industries dump their wastewater—and all the chemicals and toxins it contains—directly into local waterways.

## Climate Change

For the past 200 years, another kind of human activity has been disrupting the water cycle—burning **fossil fuels**.

Fossil fuels are oil, coal, and natural gas. We rely on them to power cars, planes, boats, and other types of transportation. We use them to operate machinery and to heat factories and homes. When they burn, these fuels release gases like carbon dioxide into our air.

Toxic waste water flowing directly into a stream from an industrial plant.

The dry lakebed of Big Bear Lake in California (upper left) stands in stark contrast to a photo (above) of the same lake taken several years ago. As of late 2014, all of California has been in the most severe stages of drought. Warmer temperatures may also cause polar ice, such as this glacier in Antarctica (left), to melt at a faster rate.

Earth's atmosphere acts like a garden greenhouse and has always contained these gases. They keep the planet warm and able to support life. The more fossil fuels we burn, though, the more of these gases go into our atmosphere. This changes the natural balance of these gases and puts all life forms at risk.

When the concentration of these gases increases, Earth's atmosphere starts to act even more like a greenhouse, trapping more and more of the Sun's heat. Just like the air in a greenhouse, the temperature inside our atmosphere becomes warmer than it should naturally be. This is called **climate change**, and the gases are called greenhouse gases.

Warmer temperatures mean glaciers and Arctic ice melt more quickly than is natural, causing ocean levels to rise. Higher temperatures may also lead to drought, which prevents crops from growing properly. Lakes and rivers can dry up, meaning the supply of fresh water decreases. Rising global temperatures also lead to unusual weather patterns and natural disasters. Hurricanes,

# Algae in Bloom

Fertilizers that farmers use to grow food are one of the biggest threats to our waterways.

Fertilizers are full of an element called nitrogen. Nitrogen helps plants grow healthy and strong. Eventually, though, rain and watering of plants wash fertilizer, with its excess nitrogen, into local bodies of water.

This nitrogen helps some aquatic plants grow. Unfortunately, it's not such a good thing for other species that live in the same bodies of water.

Algae are plant-like, but not true plants. These organisms can be as small as a single cell or as large as giant seaweed. When nitrogen washes into the water, algae thrive. They grow so fast that they form a sort of carpet across the top of the water. This is called an **algal bloom**.

The algal bloom blocks sunlight from plants in the water. Without sunlight, plants cannot thrive. In addition, when all the algae die, they rot and take oxygen out of the water. Without oxygen, animals in the water will die.

Tourists swim in water full of seaweed in the Yellow Sea, off of China. Algal blooms like this can spread from fresh water into oceans. They consume large quantities of oxygen, thus threatening to **suffocate** aquatic plants and animals.

wildfires, and lightning storms may not appear to be related to global warming and other forms of climate change, but they are.

Some greenhouse gases enter the water cycle when it rains. They mix with the water as it condenses to form acids. When this falls to Earth in raindrops, we call the rainfall **acid rain**. Acid rain can kill plants and make lakes and rivers too acidic for certain marine creatures.

The good news today is that scientists recognize that all these human activities are causing problems for our world in general, and our water in particular. They are working on ways to help put the water cycle back on track.

# CHAPTER 6

# Working for Water

On its own, the water cycle would naturally stay in balance and be healthy. Unfortunately, it can't keep up with all the stresses that humans are placing on it. It has been diverted, polluted, and taken for granted for so long that in some parts of the world it is in crisis. Some places have too little water. Others have water, but it's too dirty to drink. In some areas, there is drought. In others, there is flooding. When the water cycle doesn't follow its natural flow, it affects all life on Earth. Fortunately, groups are working to educate people about how the water cycle works and how to be sure that the water they drink is clean and safe. Also, scientists and engineers are working hard to help get the water cycle back on track.

A farmer in India sits in the middle of his rice crop during a severe drought. With no means of irrigation, or channeling water to his field from a remote source, he has little choice but to sit and wait for rain.

## Rainmakers

Hydrologists are scientists who study water and the water cycle. Some of them could also be called rainmakers, because they are working on ways to make it rain in dry places.

The most common technique used to increase rainfall is called "cloud seeding." In this method, scientists spray particles of certain chemicals into clouds. Sometimes, they shoot the particles from the ground. Other times they release them from airplanes. The idea is that water droplets in the air will attach to the particles. When the watery particles become too heavy to stay in the air, they fall as rain.

In another technique, scientists shoot electrically charged particles into clouds. The energy in these particles draws droplets of water together to form drops heavy enough to fall as rain.

Cloud-seeding equipment mounted on the wing of a plane. The tubes, known as "flares," are similar to highway flares. They shoot out chemical solutions or even gas cylinders designed to clump water droplets into larger drops, which will then fall as rain.

## MAKING SENSE OF CYCLES

Scientists are working on ways to increase rainfall in dry areas and remove salt from ocean water in places where there is a shortage of fresh water. Their goals include relieving drought, improving growing conditions, and helping people who don't have clean water to drink. But some people think we should not try to tamper with the weather. Why do you think people oppose these activities? Do you feel that we should or should not manipulate weather conditions? Based on things you have read in this book about the effects that humans have had on the water cycle, explain your thoughts.

China is the country that does the most cloud seeding, but the United States and Russia have also been doing it since the 1950s.

Other groups of scientists are working toward increasing the world's drinking water supply by removing salt from ocean water. This is called desalination. One desalination technique involves forcing water through a membrane, or screen, with **microscopic** pores. This allows the water molecules through, but not the salt molecules. In another method, salt water is heated, and the water evaporates. The pure water vapor is then cooled, condensed, and collected. The salt is left behind. The Middle East produces the most desalinated water in the world.

## Cleaning Up

While some scientists and engineers are working on ways to increase available drinking water, others are looking for ways to clean up dirty water.

Many countries are making laws to limit air and water pollution. The goal is to slow down or stop the harmful activities of industry, transportation, shipping, and urban living.

Some scientists are studying new ways to purify water for drinking. They are looking into new filtration techniques and experimenting with ultraviolet light that will kill harmful bacteria in water. Others are researching different ways to clean industrial wastewater, and even sewage, so that it becomes drinkable.

This seawater desalination plant in Israel is the largest of its kind in the world. The objective of the plant is to help reduce the water shortage in this arid Middle Eastern country.

Anything you can do to reduce your water use will help keep more water flowing through the water cycle and increase your local supply of fresh, usable water. You could do these things:

• Ask the people you live with if you can time how long it takes them to brush their teeth. Then close the sink's drain with its stopper and run the water for the same amount of time. You'll be able to see and actually measure how much water went down the drain.
• Now turn the tap off when you brush your teeth!
• Ask grown-ups you know to install low-flow shower heads and faucets. These control the speed, amount, and direction of water to cut down on unnecessary flow in bathtubs and sinks.

You can help reduce water use by making sure your family only runs the washing machine or dishwasher with full loads.

• If you don't have a low-flow toilet, put a bottle filled with sand and capped in the tank so it doesn't use as much water.
• Take short showers instead of baths.
• While you're waiting for the water to warm up, place a bucket in the shower to collect the water. This water can be used to flush the toilet.
• Use soapy water from a sink or washing machine to flush the toilet.
• Sweep the sidewalk, porch, or patio rather than hosing it down.
• Carry a refillable water bottle rather than buying bottled water.
• Encourage the adults in your life to wash their cars less often and to use a bucket rather than a hose.
• If you live in a dry area, choose plants that are drought tolerant. This means that they are naturally adapted to dry and drought conditions. A good place to start in any area is with native plants—plants that are naturally perfectly suited to precipitation in your area. Check with a nearby garden center, university, museum, or parks department to learn more about native plants.
• Encourage your school to start a water conservation program.
• Research water charities to see how you can help.

Some engineers are finding new ways to build homes and factories that use less energy. Others are developing electric cars, airplanes that run on solar power, and trains that are pulled along their tracks by magnetic forces rather than being driven by fossil fuels. Others are looking into new—and renewable—sources of fuel. In addition to solar power, these potential energy sources include wind power and the movement of rising and falling tides. Researchers are also finding ways to reduce humans' use of fossil fuels.

All of these efforts will help reduce the production of greenhouse gases, and therefore reduce acid rain and climate change.

There are also many charity organizations around the world focusing on clean water. For example, an organization called FogQuest has developed a system of nets and tubes that collect the water drops in fog. Right now, fog collector systems are at work or being planned in several countries.

## MAKING SENSE OF CYCLES

This house in Melbourne, Australia, was designed with a system that harvests as much rainwater as possible from the roof and other parts of the building. The water is stored in a tank and can be used for a variety of household purposes.

Ask your family to consider buying a rain barrel to collect rainwater. (It doesn't have to be as fancy as this one!) How might this help make the water cycle flow more smoothly, help save water, and keep our supply of water fresh, safe, and clean? Based on what you have learned in this book about water and the water cycle, come up with a list of uses for the water collected in the rain barrel.

These include Chile, Guatemala, Morocco, Ethiopia, Eritrea, Nepal, Yemen, and Israel. These countries are all at high risk for poor-quality or inadequate supplies of fresh water. A single fog collector gathers an average of 53 gallons (200 liters) a day. Other charity groups are digging wells, donating portable water filters, building sanitation systems, and educating people about water-safety issues.

The water cycle will never stop working. It just needs our help. The more we understand the problems that human activities are creating for the water cycle, the more we can do to help it find its flow.

The nets in this FogQuest system in Yemen capture the water droplets that make up fog. The open-topped tubes at the bottom of the nets collect the clean water dripping from the nets and channel it to receptacles on or in the ground.

# Moving Around the Water Cycle

You have learned that all of Earth's water moves through the water cycle. In a very simple example, the Sun shines on the surface of the ocean. Water on the surface evaporates and rises as water vapor into the air. The water vapor cools, condenses, and gathers in droplets to form clouds. When the water droplets get heavy enough, they fall back to Earth as precipitation. Those that do not fall into a body of water may make their way down hillsides as surface runoff or seep into the ground as groundwater. Eventually, most of the water that falls back to Earth reaches the sea.

**Can we observe all the stages of the water cycle up close?**

In this activity, you will design a working model of the water cycle that includes all four stages: evaporation, condensation, precipitation, and collection.

## You Will Need

- Clear quart-size (946-mL) plastic self-sealing bag (no writing on sides)
- Fine point permanent marker
- 3-ounce (88.7-mL) transparent plastic bathroom cup
- Water
- Masking tape
- Notebook or pad of paper and pen or pencil
- Blue food coloring (optional)
- Notebook or pad of paper and pen or pencil

## Instructions

**1** Turn your plastic bag at an angle (diamond shape) so one corner points up and the opposite corner points down.

**2** Using the diamond shape as a guide, draw a model of the water cycle in your notebook. Label all four parts: evaporation, condensation, precipitation, collection. Add arrows to show the direction that the water moves through the cycle.

Water Cycle

**3** Use marker to copy your water cycle drawing and labels onto one side of the plastic bag. Add mountains, clouds, and other features as you wish.

**4** Fill the cup 1/3 full of water. Mark the water line on the outside of the cup.

**5** Holding the bag by the upper corner, carefully tuck the cup upright into the lower corner so it doesn't tip.

**7** Still holding the bag by the top corner, use strips of masking tape to tape it securely onto the inside of a sunny window.

**6** Seal the bag so it is closed tightly. Leave enough air inside so the sides aren't touching.

**8** Check on your water cycle bag once an hour. In your notebook, use words and drawings to record what you see happening.

**9** Continue to observe your water cycle bag occasionally over the next four days, recording what you see.

## The Challenge

After several days, present your model to others, explaining what you did, how it works, and what you have discovered. Think about and discuss:

- How this model represents Earth's water cycle.
- How this model is different from Earth's water cycle.
- What changes you noticed in the water level in the cup.
- Predict what might happen if you put blue food coloring in the water in the cup. What color would the collection water be? Start this model over or set up a new one to find out.
- Explain why the cycle inside the bag created more condensation at some times than at others.

# GLOSSARY

**abundant**  Plentiful

**acid rain**  Rainfall produced by certain chemicals in the atmosphere combined with rain to make it more acidic

**algal bloom**  An area where algae have grown so quickly that they form a sort of carpet over the water, blocking sunlight from entering the water below

**altitude**  The height of something in relation to ground or sea level

**aquatic**  Of or relating to water

**aquifer**  An underground layer or pocket of fresh water

**atmosphere**  The layer of gases surrounding Earth

**atoms**  The basic unit of a chemical element. Atoms make up all living and nonliving things

**climate change**  The gradual increase in the temperature of Earth's atmosphere due to the increased levels of greenhouse gases

**collection**  A step in the water cycle in which water is collected and stored on Earth

**compound**  Atoms and molecules that bond together to form a new substance

**concentration**  The amount of a chemical or substance dissolved in water (or other liquid)

**condensation**  The process of converting, or changing, a substance from a gaseous state to a liquid state

**contaminated**  Made impure by the introduction of or exposure to a poisonous or polluting substance

**deposition**  The process of depositing something

**dew**  Tiny drops of water that form on cool surfaces at night when vapor condenses

**drought**  A prolonged period with little to no rainfall which results in a shortage of water

**element**  A pure chemical substance. Each element contains only one type of atom

**evaporation**  The process of converting, or changing, a substance from a liquid to a gaseous state. For example, when water evaporates, it becomes water vapor

**fossil fuel**  A fuel source that began as organisms or plant material buried deep beneath Earth's surface underwent decomposition and other natural processes, usually over periods of millions of years, and were eventually converted to oil, coal, or natural gas

**fresh water**  Water that is not salt water, or ocean water

**gaseous**  Of or relating to the state of being a gas. For example, water vapor is the form of water in its gaseous state

**groundwater**  Fresh water that has soaked into the ground

**impurity**  A substance, such as dirt or bacteria, that differs from the chemical composition of a material

**microscopic**  So small as to be visible only with a microscope

**molecule**  A particle formed when two or more atoms bond together

**nutrient**  A substance that provides nourishment that is necessary for growth and for life, such as a vitamin or a mineral

**oasis**  A spot in a desert where water is found

**parasite**  An organism that lives on or inside another organism; the parasite gets its food from its host, usually at the expense of the host

**Periodic Table of Elements**  A table that shows all known chemical elements, in order of atomic number, or the number of protons in the atom's nucleus

**photosynthesis**  A process by which plants convert carbon dioxide, water, and sunlight into oxygen and sugars

**pollutant**  Something that contaminates air, water, or a place with foreign or poisonous substances

**precipitation**  A step in the water cycle in which water falls from the sky to the ground as rain, snow, hail, or sleet

**proton**  A positively charged particle in the nucleus of an atom

**reservoir**  An artificial, or human-made, body of water used to store fresh water for a city or town

**runoff**  Water that trickles down hillsides or rocks or along pavement without sinking into the ground

**saturated**  Full; thoroughly soaked with liquid so no more can be absorbed

**scarcity**  A shortage of something, usually so not enough is available to satisfy demand

**sublimation**  The change of the state of water from solid to gas without going through its liquid phase

**suffocate**  To die due to lack of oxygen

**surface water**  Water that collects on the surface of the ground

**thermal pollution**  The degradation or pollution of water by raising its temperature higher than it would naturally be

**transpiration**  Giving off water vapor through stomata in the leaves of a plant

**water table**  The underground level below which the ground is saturated with, or full of, water

**water vapor**  Water in its gaseous state

## BOOKS

Morgan, Sally. *The Water Cycle* (Nature's Cycles). New York: Rosen Publishing Group, 2009.

Mulder, Michelle. *Every Last Drop: Bringing Clean Water Home* (Orca Footprints). Victoria, British Columbia, Canada: Orca Book Publishers, 2014.

Trueit, Trudi Strain. *The Water Cycle* (Watts Library). New York: Franklin Watts, 2002.

## WEBSITES

**eschooltoday.com/pollution/water-pollution/what-is-water-pollution.html**
Everything you need to know about water pollution is on this colorful website. It is called *Your Cool Facts and Tips About Water Pollution*. It presents causes and effects of water pollution, along with solutions to pollution problems and other resources

**www.creditvalleyca.ca/watershed-science/our-watershed/the-water-cycle/how-humans-affect-the-water-cycle/**
Excellent video showing why we should care about water.

**www.environment.nationalgeographic.com/environment/freshwater/**
National Geographic produces excellent collections of stories, videos, and photographs on a variety of subjects. This link takes you to the main subject page for *Freshwater*. From here, you can click through to pages on everything from frogs, turtles, and dolphins, to drought, flooding, and the impact of oil spills. The link to The American Nile (about the Colorado River) is a multi-media must-see! Here it is: **www.nationalgeographic.com/americannile/**

There are many excellent organizations around the world dedicated to water. Here are a few for you to research, but maybe your own city or town has its own water project that needs your help!

**water.org/**
**http://thewaterproject.org/**
**www.waterislife.com/**
**www.charitywater.org**

## ABOUT THE AUTHOR

Diane Dakers was born and raised in Toronto, and now makes her home in Victoria, British Columbia, Canada. She has been a newspaper, television, and radio journalist since 1991. She lives on an island, surrounded by seawater, in a region where it rains a lot.